To Bloom, To Wilt, To be Reborn Again

Angela Carreon

Presentation by *BookLeaf Publishing*

Web: www.bookleafpub.com

E-mail: info@bookleafpub.com

ISBN: 9789358369670

First edition 2023

DEDICATION

I dedicate this book to myself, to bloom, to wilt,
to be reborn again.

ACKNOWLEDGEMENT

I'd like to acknowledge my friend Maya, who brought up this opportunity to get the chance to publish this book. She is also an amazing writer. I met her through my writing club that she was the president of, Maya I adore you so much. I'd also like to thank my Aunt-mom who has supported me in every way since the moment I was placed into her care. Ruby, thank you for pushing me towards school and always making sure I was getting good grades. Lastly, to my friends and family who have gotten to read my work, thank you for making me smile with your reactions and sweet words.

PREFACE

Within this book lie pieces of myself, whether they are experiences or various feelings. Almost my entire being is within these words I've put together, and whatever interpretation you have for each poem, I hope you connect with it on a personal level. You may prefer my own meaning or another; however, it really doesn't matter. I believe meaning in creative pieces is subjective, just like beauty. There is no right or wrong answer, just a preference. In these poems, I have a different theme of love, my life, and a story.

May I?

One day
On my walk
I searched for a flower
Just one
For my sweet lover
Whose favorite flower
Was a rose

Red and delicate
Tall and perfect
Just like her
A beautiful classic
So as I walked
Right off the sidewalk
I found a garden
Where I had to bargain
With the lady of the garden

I asked politely
For admission
To her beautiful garden
With her gracious permission
Yet the lady laughed
And she waved me in
With no second thought
I thanked her anyway
Despite giving her
A confused glance
And walked straight in

The garden was a beauty
Luscious in greenery
Heavy with all of nature's finery
So many pickings
Of fruits, weeds, and flowers
I wish I could stay and stare
Yet I was only there

For just one flower

Pushing past my admiration
I began to follow my determination
Looking through rose bushes
White, pink, and yellow
Yet no red
Orange and green
I'm filling with dread
Blue and black
Oh my, where is red?
Purple lavenders
I rushed past
Oh
Red, there is red

A rose bush filled with shiny
Ruby reds
Glittering with great immense
Beauty, perfection, and delicacy
A classic red
Just like my lover
I knew one was all I needed
And only one stood out to me
Right in the middle
My eyes shot at it like a missile

At once I ran to the lady
Asking for the rose

Hoping she'd give me
If I was full of pity
But the lady smiled
She found me amusing
Saying I couldn't ask her
But the rose itself
Bewildered I was
Daring I was not
Why question the lady
Who was of the garden?

To the rose I faced
Perfect with no disgrace
I dared not waste
The time I had to make
For the rose's beauty
Was no mistake
I asked the rose
May I take you home?
Your perfect
And will never be alone
The rose said nothing
Leaving me quite frightened
So I waited
Not wanting to be unenlightened

I felt the need to ask again
But then
I heard a giggle

Where the rose began
You want to take me home?
By ripping me away from my home?
How dare you ask, me as a rose
To be plucked and dethroned
My placing as the best rose?

I was stunned
But I needed this rose
So I asked again
Oh rose, I'm sorry
But please at least let me beg
Plead and have you forgive the wreck
That I am
For you are perfect, delicate, and
Unforgettably red
My lover would be so happy
To have a rose
As fine as you

The rose was silent again
It did not scoff
Nor did it giggle
But it did hum
With a bit of surprise
Is your lover as perfect as me?
Delicate and tall?
Does your lover look good in red?
I nodded, quite excitedly

I promise you
That you, rose
Will feel like your just at home
Right by the side
Of my lover
Perfect as you
So may I?

The rose at last
Agreed for me
To take it home
As the lady of the garden
Who allowed me to roam
Waved me goodbye
And watched me go
So I walked along hills
While my heart began to fill
As I got closer to see my lover
Tall and perfect
Never changing
A classic
Engraved in stone
Where I
Had placed the rose
Right into the ground
Beside my lover
She will never suffer
Not after I have placed
The rose that I discovered.

Plucked

She felt comfortable
In the grass carpet
Roots tangled
And buried

Being grounded
Was her favorite thing
Since
She never wanted
to be plucked

Yet she rose
While her petals fell
With her thorns
Eating away at my hands

I took
She fought
I plucked
And she rot
Wilting with love me's
And love me not's

Yet it was all
For nought
For she did not
love me

She loved the ground
Her thirst
And richness
Of her velvety petals

But now
She is gone
Dead and all
Yet still
As beautiful
As the day
I plucked her

Oh How I Fell

The time had came
Where I slipped
And fell
For the woman of hell
How beautiful she was
Her tale
Now I will gladly tell

The description of my infliction
Would be filled
With only mindless affection
Tangled in underlying
Friction

Yet I reveled
In her smile
Being of a little devil
Eager for my soul
Towering my easel
Of shyful upheaval

Oh how
She painted me
In reds, blues, and purples
Feathering kisses
Upon my arrival

I wonder of the days
We had spent
Wrapping each other
In arms and legs
Finding ourselves so close
In every second
Every minute
And every moment
Of the time we had spent

I do feel myself
Getting rather embarrassed
Yet there is no shame in love
However
I'd never thought I would fall
So far
Into the mouth of a devil

My wings were ripped
My purity stripped
By a woman's smile
Who was incredibly wild

To think it's believed
I would have to fall again
Is a chance
I might just miss
But I can't say it's unimaginable
For falling once
Was once inconceivable

My Body of Tacs

Forgive my lack
Of words that slack
For you rack
My entire body of tacs

I see the way you look
And my you are pretty
But I
Simply
Do not have the ability
To make myself

Appear flirty

My body is made of tacs
In which they all
Stick out in different ways
And clatter
When I dare speak

I hope you understand
Even in ways
Where I cannot stand
The way I fumble
My words
And senses

I am not one
That is sly
And I will never pry
But I will try
To make you smile
In the time I buy

As beautiful as you are
I wonder how far
I can take
My body of tacs
To know you
Forevermore

Careful, Love

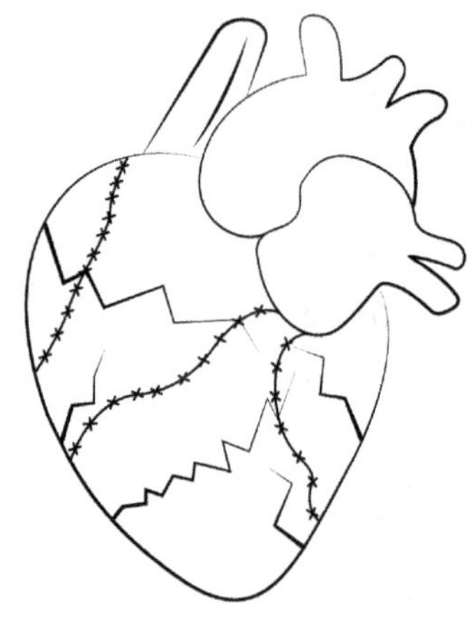

My love was hesitant
Fumbling and ever so unsure
Yet it was there
Always ready
To be spared

And I was always willing to share
Allowing those who cared
To let themselves
Feel cared for

But in life
I have those
Who took my love
Happily and carelessly
Claiming to be grateful
And ever so hopeful
To have more of my love
So I gave

I gave more and more
Hoping
That it was more than enough
To have nothing left
But just myself

Many would say
Careful, love
You have such careful love
So be careful
With all your love

Yet I kept on giving
I didn't think I'd run out
I just wanted
To love unconditionally
But then
I grew tired

I couldn't love

Not just those around me
But I couldn't love me
I grew distant
Too cautious
Too careful

I loved less
I loved in lies
I loved myself as second

I became
Careful, love
So now when I do love again
I wonder
How much more will they take?
And do I
Have to be careful, love?

Divine Feminine Energy

Oh my
Oh my
Her skin
The way it feels
So soft
So warm
Almost like velvet
Yet so much better

And I could never
Fathom

Her complete beauty
Soaked in divinity
Rich in feminine
Divine energy

Yet I wonder
How could she
Be so pretty?
So kind?
So caring?
And so unbelievably daring?

And in trying
For these trying times
I desperately desire
Her hands of fire

I wish for her lips
Soft and needy
Grabbing at mine
Holding me steady

If anything
A woman as daring as she
Could take me
With no plea
For she
Is divine feminine energy

Our Moment

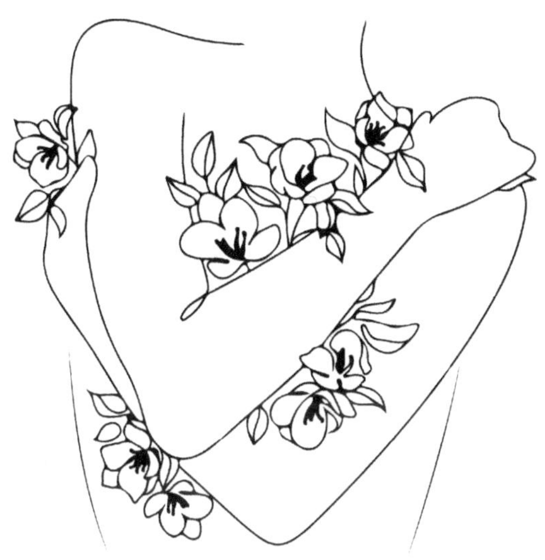

I fantasize
Your body
And hers
Against mine
So tightly compacted
Preacted
With no practice

Its like our bodies
Were made
Perfectly
To fit

Within
Each other

Encased with warmth
Soft and comforting
Time stopping
Waiting
For our moment

Our sign of high
Rising and rising
So unforgettably hot
Sweat forming
Unnoticed
Till our movement
Disruptive
To this very moment

And I could die in this moment
With no regret
To just be filled
With pure bliss
Where I
Could never miss
Anything that came before
For this moment
Is all I know
And all I can feel.

My Mirror

Mirror oh mirror
I love my mirror
She smiles at me
Telling me how much
She loves my beauty here

I carry her everywhere
Small and compacted
Right in my purse
Ready to rehearse
For a smile
To disperse

Oh how my mirror
My mirror
Never begins to leer
Although her glass is sheer
She is my precious peer
I love my mirror
My beautiful dear

At times
When I begin to tear
My mirror
She smiles
Even when my tears
Are never ending
My mirror smiles

Then she speaks
She reminds me how pretty I am
She tells me I'm perfect
She tells me I feel just enough

I could never be angry at my mirror
She is far too sweet
And far too clear
I love my mirror
So I'll always smile
Just to have her smile
My beautiful mirror

Sharp

Her touch graces my skin
With a slice and a dice
Which was nice
Till I needed to be iced
But everything about her
Was sharp, clean, and precise

And I was perfectly
Sizably cuttable
Being soft, round, and moldable
But to perfectly describe her

Would be anything but

Her nails were pointed
And her tongue split
With curves jagged
Honing the inability
To be coddled

As her lips curved
Into sharp ends
Her teeth peeked
As sharped dead ends
Twisting her features
Into fractures

Which was wild
And precisely sharp
And with no doubt
Could she tear me apart

Yet I sit still
As I embrace her sharped ends
Creating pristine cuts
Along my skin
Being sharp, clean, and precise

Lilly's Waters

As I bathe
In the waters of my own disposal
I lay there
Being entirely composable

Yet I notice
The ripples of water
Created at my fingertips
Where I realize

My essence
Is offering penance

My blood is mixing
With the water
Running so unbearably cold
My significance becoming dull

But what could I have done wrong?
When the weight of my body
Floating, ever so lightly
Guilt flaring sparsely

The water had rebirth me
For all my sins
Washed for absence
I'm good licensed

So I ask again
What could I have done wrong?
When I match the delicacy
Of a Lilly
So innocently strong

To Breathe

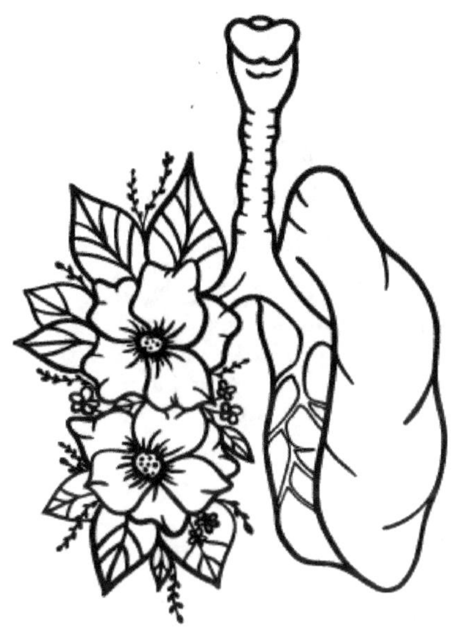

It may be strange
But I find myself suffocating
A little too often
It's stuffy in every room
So I have to open every window
And leave my fan on
For every hour of the day

It's the wind. I think it's the wind
The fresh air

Or perhaps it's the cold
Either way
I just love to breathe it in
It's incredibly refreshing

I guess it's a bit silly
To enjoy breathing
Well, of course I love to breathe
How else could I stay alive?
But that's the point
I love being alive

To be able to fill my lungs
To then exhale
To where I am free
To be able to breathe

I would always hold my breath
Refuse to let out a word or thought
To stay suffocating
Yet here I am
Breathing freely
Where I finally
Get to love to breathe

What Color Could I Be?

I want to be pretty
Like the color pink

Soft and ditty
While being a little witty

But I'm more of a red
That's rotted
And dried into a brown
Wondering
Why do I
Have to keep my head down?

So now
I wish I was a yellow
Happy and mellow
Flowing in the wind
Like the life of a willow

Yet I'm more of a blue
Hollowing out
Weeping
Searching to be
Something completely
Brand new

I wonder if I
Could be an orange
Always smiling
Bright in the summers
Tasting sweet and sour
Looking up

In its tangy attitude

But then again
I'm more of a red
Changing in shades
Wanting to be bold
Deep in color

Furious and growing loud
Only to calm
Healing into
A light shade
Of pink

Bound to Sound

The beauty of solitude
Is found when listening
To silence
For it is a sound
Cozy when welcomed

However, I cannot welcome such a sound
In fact
I despise it
Simply because
I can not welcome it

Not while I eat
Not while I'm alone
Not while I'm awake

Whenever silence comes around
I find it hard
To accept it with open arms
I need sound
To always surround
So I can be bound

Never will I
Be encased
In silence
My mind is far too loud
Always talking
And always craving
Someone to talk to

Yes I enjoy solitude
But never the silence that comes along side it
It's especially horrible
Silence is there

Even when I am not alone

Why sit in silence
When you can hear
Every sound
Of being alive?

Even then, complete silence
Surely cannot exist
Not while you stand
Awake and alive

You are your own sound
Why waste it
For being the sound of silence?

A Catwalk

In lives
I have nine
Forever mine
And I walk a very thin line
Between life and death

Many like me
Many hate me
But all I know
Is that I am a bit curious
Perhaps mysterious

While
Gracefully I walk

Alongside a man
Whose robe is black
Finding my many lives
Quite a mind boggling
Wreck

With each life I live
I get more reckless
Frisky and mischievous
Yet I can't help it
The power I have
With the lives
Of the number of nine

I'll run across streets
Dodging cars
Eating pretty flowers
That are not mine
How silly I am
Aren't I?

Then with my claws
I will climb
Places I
Do not belong
Then I will taunt
Those who do not want
To play my silly antics

I am above god and all
For who has
The amount of lives
That I have?
Where nine
Turns into eight
To seven
To six
But I am not done
Not when I have five

Where I will have highs
To the point no one will find
Where I lie
To four
To three
I am quite daring
To still have more
Than all the ones before me

Then I have two
Yet I'm still better than you
And the line I walk
Is very thin
Right between life and death
Where now I have one
Which leaves me to question
Have I won?

La Belleza de mi Abuela

Mi abuela es bella
Habla en belleza
En que no entiende
O sabe todo
Pero yo no hablo en belleza
Hablo en cortés y preocupaciones
Donde no entiendo

Sus ojos son viejos y sabios
Mientras las mías están cansadas

Ella dice que ve belleza
Yo digo que veo preocupación
Pienso que es triste, es melancolía
Pero sonriere
Para enseñarle belleza
Aunque su belleza está floreciendo
Desbordante
Y infinitamente
Que distrae y se avecina

Me pregunto si el mio sera igual
Tal vez siempre cambiando
Pero cada vez que la veo
Siempre es igual
Nomas el tiempo pasando

Y sus manos correosas
Su empuñadura consuela
Como adoro su amor
Eso nunca termina
Porque ella es belleza
Vieja y perfecta
Disfrazado en años
De bondad sin esfuerzo

Escapist

My hands have always felt tense
My fingers too straight
Stuck in place
When I begin to crave
Things I cannot have
They curve into claws
As I scratch my arms

Where I've noticed
I begin to want more
The more I grow
Yet all I ever get told
Is what I can't have
So here I am
Wanting more
Stuck in place
Tense and feeling
Rather displaced

And now
I feel the greatest need
To escape
But in my place
I must resist
Or I will be
The greatest disgrace

My peers
They will fear me
Consider me troubled
Label me as escapist
Finding me pretentious
To escape
The home
They've all glorified

But I am horrified
To find everything
Demoralized
And I ask my peers
Aren't you mortified?
To be confined and
Dehumanized?

Yet they leer at me
Question my faith
Point and call me filth
Immediately I shut my mouth
It's no use
They do not want the things I want
The things I crave

Now I stay
My hands tense
Shaking
And wanting
For an escape

Regina George

I think this is new
I'm excited
But maybe overused
Disguised with topics
Infused with prospects
Unknowingly waiting
For unneeded gossip

Intoxicating venom
Of spitting sound

Hurting
taking
around
My moral ground

Please override me
My judgment is destructive
But what I think
Is what I'll see
All Rumored to be
Inscribed in pink
Burning in casualty

Unfortunately
It's all unforgiving
My plastic exterior
Is only following
My plastic interior
But now I am melting
Reeking of chemicals
And rumors of what I was
But never what I could be

Soured

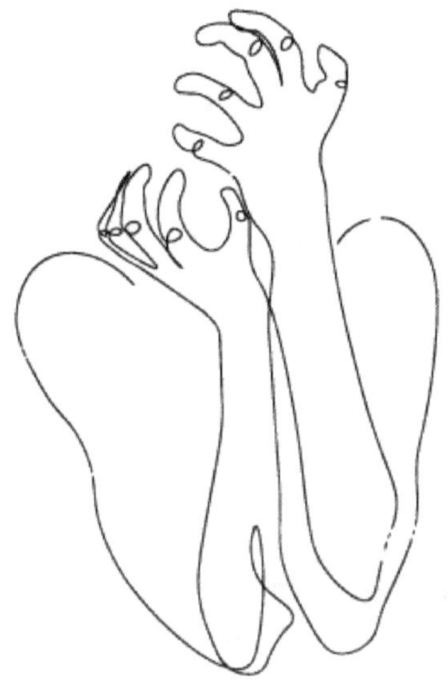

To remember the things she said
How they sounded
How they felt
So unsightly
They've become so sickly
To think they were sweet nothings
To now be rotten
Sounding like profanity

Every remembrance of touch
Makes me shiver

With loss and disgust

To see open acts of love
Only turns my stomach
With the wish
Of having my neck wrung

My love turned sour
My effort and drive
Have gone dry
The thought of retrying
Sounds mad
How could I?

I gave it my all
I had given everything to her
I laid there open and vulnerable
Always wondering
Was it enough?
Now I have nothing left

Except for bits of my pride
That I kept so close by
She hated it
To see me stubborn
Yet she was stubborn too
So much so
That she got what she wanted

A bit of my heart
A bit of mind
Body
And Soul
It was all her's
And I stupidly gifted it
With excitement
All so I
Could be left with resentment

Stickers

Simple little things
Seem to lie
In the early days
More than now

Where our smiles
Came easy
By small pictures
You can place anywhere

To the walls
To car windows

And the dashboard
Sticking them everywhere
If you were lucky enough
To not get caught

Adults however
Would soon get angry
Rambling about how hard
It would be
To take off
Those dumb little pictures

But to you
As a child
Those simple little stickers
Were nice
And brought an easy smile

Those stickers could probably stay
On the walls in secret places
When the adults wouldn't clean it up
Or decided they could stay

So when years pass by
And now you're the adult
You find the secret places
To become rather obvious

Those same little pictures

Are faded and peeling
Being not so sticky
Yellowing from time
Even ripped up
From failed attempts of removal

You probably don't even remember
Putting it there
Yet it wouldn't matter
Because your hand reaches out
Reminding you
Of your past
Gracing you
With an easy smile.